The Knight

Warfare by Duct Tape

DISCLAIMER AND TERMS OF USE AGREEMENT

ISBN-13:978-1-942006-07-7

Table of Contents

"Had I sons I should train them as your husband intends to train your son. It may be that he will never be called upon to draw a sword, but the time he has spent in acquiring its use will not be wasted. These exercises give firmness and suppleness to the figure, quickness to the eye, and briskness of decision to the mind. A man who knows that he can at need defend his life if attacked, whether against soldiers in the field or robbers in the street, has a sense of power and self-reliance that a man untrained in the use of the strength God has given him can never feel. I was instructed in arms when a boy, and I am none the worse for it."

- G. A. Henty
St. Bartholomew's Eve

The Weapons

One-Hand Sword

The one-hand sword was used by infantry. Sometimes an archer would have a sword by his side in case he had to fight in close quarters. This particular weapon was effective at such a range. It could be drawn and wielded quickly because it was of no extensive length or weight. It was called the one-hand sword because it was easy to use with only one hand.

Zweihander

The zweihander, a late medieval weapon, was extremely long and heavy. It was necessary to use two hands when fighting with this sword. It was used principally by the Germans, which explains the German name. A version of this sword was used by the Scottish for centuries and was called the claymore.

Dagger

This type of weapon has been used for centuries. As much a tool as a weapon, it rose in popularity with the invention of chainmail and at close quarters was one of the only weapons effective against it. During the medieval era, this was used for eating instead of a fork!

Spear

This weapon is as old as time. A version of it was used by knights when charging into battle. This spear design is based off of the infantry style rather than the cavalry style, although it was used by both.

Spiked Battle Axe

The spiked battle axe was often used by heavy cavalry against heavy cavalry because it was effective against most armor. The weight of the weapon could crush through plate armor and chainmail. The spike does very little but was added for ornamentation to give it a more intimidating appearance.

Halberd

The halberd is an infantry version of the spiked battle axe. The battle axe handle was lengthened to increase leverage thus increasing the force of the blows. It was widely used in the late medieval era by many cultures. This was an upgrade to the pikes that the Swiss used in the late medieval era. The Vatican Guard in Rome still use this weapon to this day.

War Hammer

The war hammer was used almost exclusively by knights. This was a specialist weapon that could be used to pierce armor with its thin, but strong, blade. Though not often used, it was rather effective. Knights would often go for the easy-to-use sword or spiked battle axe, instead of the war hammer.

Mace

The mace was used from very ancient times. It predated swords in the Bronze Age. During the Iron Age, it lost popularity to the sword. But during the medieval age it regained popularity and became widely used due to its great effectiveness against all types of armor.

Flail

The flail is an adaptation of the mace. A chain was added between the handle and the spiked weight to give it much greater power and leverage. This was a truly fearsome and dangerous weapon, although it required great skill to use.

Shield

Norman Shield

The Normans originally used round shields, but when they started riding horses into battle, they lengthened the bottom of the shield to give more protection to the rider's leg. The Norman shield was approximately 5 feet long and 2-3 feet at its widest point. In 1,066 A.D., the Normans used this shield in the conquest of England against the Saxons. Painted with artistic designs, it was made of wood with a metal boss.

Medieval Shield

Smaller than the Norman shield, this particular shield was a favorite to the armies of Christendom during the 12th-13th centuries. The top of the shield is straight and curves down to a point at the bottom resembling a triangle. It was about 3 feet long by 2 feet wide. Painted with the knight's coat of arms, this shield was wooden and had no metal boss.

Description of the Battle Game

Battling is at least two teams fighting each other using weapons. We suggest using our foam weapons to minimize injuries.

Divide your players into two teams of about the same strength and even numbers. Say there are four big guys and four little guys. There should be two big guys and two little guys on each team.

Weather is no deterrent to battling. We have had battles in rain and heat.

Object of the game: divide and conquer your enemy!

More than one battle can be played. It is important to keep score of who wins each battle. The one who wins the most battles is the victor!

You can use fortifications. Tree houses work well. Piles of logs or even swing sets can be used.

Naval battles can be fought using non-motor boats such as canoes and row boats. To fight a naval battle, simply row up to them and fight them. Do not use throwing axes, they are not waterproof.

With fortifications, it is often wise to use your spear instead of your axe or sword. The spear has greater length which is helpful in forts. It is very wise to use missiles (water balloons, throwing axes, etc.) so you can bombard the enemy without having to storm the gate.

It is crucial to use shields. People who do not use shields are usually slain early in the battle and are vulnerable to throwing axes and heavy weapons such as battle axes.

Terrible war cries intimidate the enemy.

It is important to have one main leader (general). This keeps the army unified and reduces squabbles.

Rules of the Battle Game

Rule 1

Chivalry and honor must be exhibited at all times.

Rule 2

If any weapon hits your limb (for ex. arm, leg, hand), you are no longer able to use it.

If you are holding a weapon in the hand or arm that is hit, you can't keep using the weapon with that arm but could switch it to the other arm and keep fighting. If both arms are hit, you must surrender or run away.

If your leg is hit, you must limp. If both legs are hit, you must kneel or squat. If you lose all your limbs, you are doomed!

Rule 3

If you get hit in the head, neck or torso, you are officially dead and can't play until the end of the battle.

Rule 4

The only way to win a battle is when all of the enemy (other team) are dead, have surrendered or have run away (escaped).

If a team holding prisoners is defeated, the prisoners are automatically freed.

Rule 5

If someone surrenders, you can either keep them captive, (they are not allowed to escape) or release them and they are free to return to their army (team).

Rule 6

Parley~ a parley is when one or possibly two people from each team talk to each other. To start a parley, one team member must say, "Request an audience". If the other team agrees, they send a person forward to talk to the other.

It is usually used for discussing the release of prisoners by ransom or switching of players. You can be chivalrous and release prisoners. It is important to not carry weapons but must leave them behind during a parley to avoid treachery.

Rule 7

We believe that only boys should battle with other boys. Young men should practice protecting young ladies so it is not appropriate to fight them.

Rule 8

Ransom~A ransom is when a soldier who is captured is released by a payment of money. You can make your own money (see instructions). To ransom a prisoner, first call a parley and then negotiate the price. A general usually costs more than the average soldier. (This rule is optional.)

Weapon Instructions

Introduction:

PVC pipe tips: You can find PVC pipe at your local hardware store like Lowe's and Home Depot. You will need a saw to cut the PVC pipe to the correct length. If you do not have a saw, the large hardware stores will usually cut it for you.

PVC pipe insulation~the black foam stuff. We usually buy this at the same stores as the PVC pipe. We like the kind that comes in a 4 pack of 3 foot pieces.

Foam~the 2 inch thick green stuff. You can find this foam at Wal-Mart and fabric stores like JoAnn's and Hobby Lobby. It comes in small packages or in large pieces by the yard.

Cardboard: It can be difficult to cut cardboard so younger kids might need some help or supervision. In most of the pieces that use cardboard, it is important to cut the cardboard so the "ridges" (inner corrugated sections) **run across** the narrow width of the piece. This way the piece can bend properly. Check instructions before tracing the pattern onto the cardboard.

½ Width Piece of Duct Tape: Before we begin the weapon instructions, we need to define a term we will use in the book: "½ width". To make a ½ width piece of duct tape, take a piece of duct tape and tear it lengthwise (the long way). Now you have two ½ width pieces of duct tape. Sometimes, even a ¼ width piece of duct tape is used. Just tear the ½ width piece again to make the ¼ width.

Now, on to the fun!

Sword~

Materials:

3 foot piece of ¾ inch PVC pipe

3 foot piece of PVC pipe insulation
(We use 3/8" thick polyethylene foam, fits ¾" pipe)

Duct tape

Scissors

Ruler

Saw
(You may need a saw to cut the PVC to size)

Please Note: This project may require adult help to use the sharp tools.

Directions:

Cut 8 inches off of your 3 foot piece of insulation.

Next, take the larger piece of insulation and slide it down the 3-foot PVC pipe.

Leave about 1 inch extending off of the PVC at the point of the sword.

Take the 8 inch piece of insulation foam. Cut a slit 2 inches long in the center and again on the back so they line up. Don't cut on the seam. It will weaken it.

Slide the piece of foam onto the PVC pipe to form the hilt of the sword.

Crisscross the duct tape around the hilt to strengthen it.

Tape across the end of the hilt, turn and do it again. Then tape around the end to make it smooth.

Do this on both ends of the hilt.

Cover the entire hilt with duct tape.

Be sure to wrap around the pipe/ handle.

Tape the point (end) of the sword blade the same way. Wrap the duct tape around a few times to strengthen it so it won't tear during battle.

Now tape the blade. It is helpful to have another person. Start at the hilt and wrap on a slightly diagonal angle towards the tip of the blade.

Cover the handle. Cap the end just as you did with the end of the blade.

Decorate as desired. Often wealthy Knights would put a jewel in the center of the hilt.

One hand Sword~

This is a shorter sword with smaller PVC pipe and could be used with only one hand. It is suitable for smaller Knights (and kids).

Materials:

2 foot piece of **1/2** inch PVC pipe

26 inches of PVC pipe insulation

(We use 3/8" thick polyethylene foam, fits ½ " pipe)

Duct tape

Ruler

Scissors

(You may need a saw to cut the PVC to size)

      Please Note: This project may require adult help to use the sharp tools.

Directions:

Cut the pipe insulation into 3 pieces, 20", 5" and 1".

Slide the 20" piece of pipe insulation onto the PVC pipe. Leave 2" past the end of the PVC pipe.

On the 5" piece, cut a slit 1 ½" long in the center and again on the back so they line up. Don't cut on the seam. It will weaken it.

Slide the 5" piece onto the PVC pipe to form the hilt.

Using a ½ width piece of duct tape, crisscross the duct tape all the way around the hilt to strengthen it.

To cap the ends of the hilt, tape across the end of the hilt, turn and do it again. Press in the edges. Then tape, using a ½ width of duct tape, around the end to make it smooth.

Do this on both ends of the hilt.

Again, using a ½ width piece of duct tape, tape around the handle and on the blade of the one hand sword above and below the hilt.

Tape a piece of duct tape on the very center of the hilts to cover up the black insulation.

Using a ½ width piece of duct tape, tape around the hilt where any black insulation is showing through.

Put the 1 inch piece of pipe insulation on the end of the handle.

Cap the end of the handle. Wrap a piece of duct tape tightly around the base of the handle centered over the black pipe insulation (a little tape hanging off each side).

Pinch the duct tape down onto the PVC pipe.

Press in the edges of the duct tape on the very end.

Tear a square of duct tape and put it on the end.

Using a ½ width piece of duct tape, wrap around the pinched part where it meets the PVC pipe.

Cap the tip of the blade of the one hand sword by taping over the end.
Press down the edges of the duct tape.
Turn the one hand sword and tape again.
Press down the edges to give a finished look.

Now tape the blade. It is helpful to have another person to hold the roll of duct tape. Start at the hilt and wrap on a slightly diagonal angle towards the tip of the blade.

Cover any spots where the pipe insulation shows through.

Decorate the one hand sword as desired.

Zweihander~

Materials:

5 foot piece of ¾ inch PVC pipe~ lightweight

3 pieces of 3 foot PVC pipe insulation (9 feet)

(We use 3/8" thick polyethylene foam, fits ¾" pipe)

Duct tape

Ruler

Scissors

Saw (You may need a saw to cut the PVC to size)

      Please Note: This project may require adult help to use the sharp tools.

Directions:

Slide a 3 foot piece of black pipe insulation down the PVC pipe. Leave 1 ½ inches past the end of the PVC pipe.

Cut the pipe insulation into a 12 inch piece, a 9 inch piece, a 6 inch piece and a 2 inch piece.

Take the 12 inch piece and cut a 2 inch slit in the center on both sides. (It is best not to cut on the seam in the pipe insulation.) Set aside for now.

Cut a 2 inch slit in the center of the 6 inch piece of pipe insulation on both sides.

Slide the piece of 6 inch pipe insulation onto the PVC pipe to form the hilt of the sword.

Slide the 9 inch piece of pipe insulation on the PVC pipe, right up next to the 6 inch hilt.

Slide the piece of 12 inch pipe insulation onto the PVC pipe to form the second hilt of the sword

Put the 2 inch piece of pipe insulation on the end of the handle.

Using a ½ width piece of duct tape, crisscross the duct tape all the way around the hilts to strengthen them.

Again, using a ½ width piece of duct tape, tape around the handle and on the blade of the zweihander above and below the hilts.

Tape around the outer parts of the hilts.

Tape a piece of duct tape on the very center of the hilts to cover up the black insulation.

To cap the ends of the hilts, tape across the end of the hilt, turn and do it again. Use a long piece of duct tape for the longer hilt. Then tape around the end to make it smooth.

Do this on both ends of the hilt. Cover the rest of the hilt. You can spiral tape the longer hilt for a nice effect.

Cap the end of the handle. Wrap a piece of duct tape tightly around the base of the handle half way over the black pipe insulation.

Pinch the duct tape down onto the PVC pipe. Using a ½ width piece of duct tape, wrap around the pinched part.

Place a piece of duct tape over the end, press in the corners and sides. Turn and do it again with another piece of duct tape. Wrap a ½ width piece of duct tape around the end.

Cap the tip of the blade of the zweihander by taping over the end.
Press down the edges of the duct tape. Turn the zweihander and tape again. Press down the edges to give a finished look.

Now tape the blade. It is helpful to have another person to hold the roll of duct tape. Start at the hilt and wrap on a slightly diagonal angle towards the tip of the blade.

Finish covering the blade between the hilts.

Decorate the zweihander as you like!

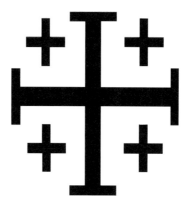

Dagger~

Materials:
6 inch piece of ¾ inch PVC pipe

8 inch piece of PVC pipe insulation

(We use 3/8" thick polyethylene foam, fits ¾" pipe)

Duct tape

Scissors/ Ruler

Saw (You may need a saw to cut the PVC to size)

Please Note: This project may require adult help to use the sharp tools.

Directions:
Slide the insulation onto the PVC pipe leaving 4 inches for the handle.

Tape across the end of the insulation at the tip of the dagger, turn and repeat. Then tape around the end to make it smooth.

Starting at the tip, wrap the duct tape on a slightly diagonal angle until the insulation is covered and just onto the PVC pipe.

 Using a ½ width piece of duct tape, tape around the base of the blade over the PVC pipe to reinforce it.

Cover handle with the color of your choice, tucking in the ends as you go. Decorate as desired.

Spear~

Materials:

4 foot piece of ¾ inch PVC pipe

1 foot piece of PVC pipe insulation

(We use 3/8" thick polyethylene foam, fits ¾" pipe)

Duct tape

Scissors/ Ruler

Saw (You may need a saw to cut the PVC to size)

Please Note: This project may require adult help to use the sharp tools.

Directions:

Slide the 1 foot piece of pipe insulation onto the PVC pipe. Leave at least 2 inches extending past the end of the PVC pipe.

Tape across the end of the insulation at the tip of the spear, turn and repeat. Then tape around the end to make it smooth.

Starting at the tip, wrap the duct tape on a slightly diagonal angle until the insulation is covered and just onto the PVC pipe.

Using a ½ width piece of duct tape, tape around the base of the blade over the PVC pipe to reinforce it.

Then, taking the color of your choice, tape a long strip down the length of the pipe. Smooth edges of tape.

Tuck end of the tape into the open end of the PVC pipe.

Repeat on the reverse side of the PVC pipe so that the handle is covered. It usually takes 2 strips of duct tape to cover the handle of the spear.

Decorate as desired.

Spiked Battle Axe~

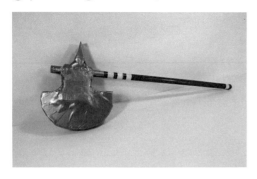

Materials:

1 piece of foam 12" by 11" by 2" thick

3 foot piece of ¾ inch PVC pipe

Cardboard 4" x 12"

Duct tape

Scissors

Marker

Pattern

Saw (You may need a saw to cut the PVC to size)

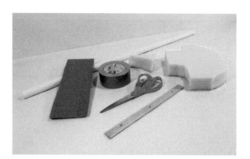

Please Note: This project may require adult help to use the sharp tools.

Directions:

Print and cut out the patterns, Spiked Battle Axe Blade and Spiked Battle Axe Spike. Lay the patterns on the foam, trace the blade of the battle axe on the foam using a permanent marker and then cut it out.   Do the same for the spike piece.

Bend the piece of cardboard in half. (See picture) Place the foam blade next to the PVC pipe about 1" down from the end. Fold cardboard over both of them and tape down the cardboard very well. Make sure to go all the way around the base of the blade.

Tape the cardboard diagonally to keep the pipe from sliding. It is best if you do it around the outside and again on the inside of the pipe.

 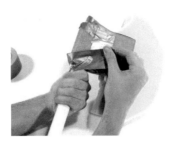 

To cap the end of the spiked battle axe, put a piece of duct tape on the end and press down the edges.

Then wrap a piece of duct tape around the end.

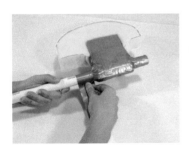

Tape over the place where the duct tape crosses the PVC pipe, below the blade.

Cover the cardboard (by the pipe) with duct tape.

Now cover the edge of the blade.

Cover the blade with duct tape piecing diagonally in a fan shape from the cardboard around the edge of the blade to the other side and up to the cardboard.

The spike:
Place the spike on the opposite side of the pipe from the blade. Attach it to the battle axe by taping a small piece to the side of the spike. Do this on both sides of the spike.

Fold down edges of the tape.

Reinforce spike by taping the ends to the pipe.

Now, tape the edge of the spike.

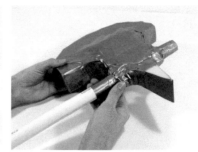

Cover the sides of the spike with duct tape. Press down the edges of the tape.

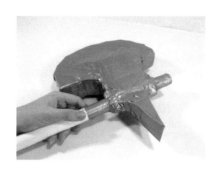

Cap the end of the handle. Place a piece of duct tape over the end. Press the edges down around the PVC pipe.

Wrap another piece of tape around the end to give a smooth finish.

Cover the handle with duct tape.

Decorate the handle as you desire.

The spiked battle axe is finished!

Halberd~

Materials:

4 foot piece of ¾ inch PVC pipe

1 foot piece of PVC pipe insulation

(We use 3/8" thick polyethylene foam, fits ¾" pipe)

1 piece 6" x 8" x 2" thick foam

Duct tape

Cardboard 3" x 3" (need 2)

Scissors/ Marker/ Ruler

Saw (You may need a saw to cut the PVC pipe to size)

   Please Note: This project may require adult help to use the sharp tools.

Directions:

Print and cut out the patterns, Halberd Blade and Halberd Spike. Lay the patterns on the foam, trace the spike and the blade on the foam using a permanent marker and then cut them out.

Slide the one foot piece of pipe insulation onto the PVC pipe, leaving an inch of foam past the end of the PVC pipe.

Tape the pipe insulation to the PVC pipe. Using a ½ width piece of duct tape, firmly tape it again.

Cap the end of the halberd by taping over the end.
Press down the edges of the duct tape. Turn the halberd and
tape again. Press down the edges to give it a finished look.

Cover the end of the halberd
with duct tape. Wrap in a spiral
direction.

Place the foam blade piece about 6 inches down from the end. Take a long piece of duct
tape and tape the blade to the shaft of the halberd, wrapping around the shaft and onto
the foam again.

Do it again.

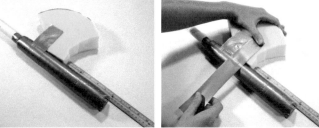

Place cardboard on the foam and overlap slightly onto the
shaft of the halberd. Using a long piece of duct tape, tape
around cardboard and foam all the way around to the other
side.

Repeat for the other side.

For extra strength, tape over
cardboard and around the shaft
using 2 pieces of duct tape.

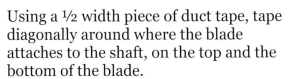

Using a ½ width piece of duct tape, tape
diagonally around where the blade
attaches to the shaft, on the top and the
bottom of the blade.

27

Tape around the shaft with a ½ width piece, above and below the blade.

Tape around the edge of the blade.

Cover the blade by placing a long piece of duct tape from the cardboard over the edge of the blade and back up to the cardboard on the other side.

Continue to cover the blade with duct tape; alternate between strengthening the edges of the blade and taping in a fan shape.

Now for the spike:

Place a piece of duct tape at the point of the spike and tape to the shaft.

Do the same on the back.

Press down the edges of the duct tape.

Tape the edge of the spike.

Tape diagonally over the edges of the spike, on the top and the bottom of the spike over the PVC pipe.

Tape around the shaft with a ½ width piece of duct tape on the top and bottom of the spike for strength.

Tape around the main part of the spike. Press down the edges of the duct tape.

Cover any foam that may be showing.

Cap the end of the halberd. Place a piece of duct tape over the end. Press the edges down around the PVC pipe.

Wrap another piece of tape around the end to give a smooth finish.

Decorate the handle as you desire. You have made a halberd!

War hammer~

Materials:

30 inch piece of ¾ inch PVC pipe

36 inch piece of PVC pipe insulation

(We use 3/8" thick polyethylene foam, fits ¾" pipe)

1 piece 7" x 4" x 2" foam

Duct tape

Ruler

Marker

Scissors

Saw

(You may need a saw to cut the PVC to size)

Please Note: This project may require adult help to use the sharp tools.

Directions:

Cut a 1 ½ inch piece of pipe insulation and slide it on the end of the PVC pipe.

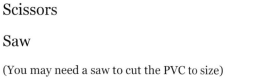

Cut a piece of pipe insulation 25 ½ inches long. Slide it on the PVC pipe (the other end). Leave 2 ½ inches past the end of the PVC pipe.

Cover the end of the war hammer with the 1 ½ inch black piece by taping over the end.
Press down the edges of the duct tape. Turn the war hammer and tape again. Press down the edges to give a finished look.

Wrap the end with a piece of duct tape. Pinch the edge onto the PVC pipe.

Using a ½ width of duct tape, tape around the handle just above the end piece.

Tape the pipe insulation to the PVC pipe, just above the handle. Press down the tape. Using a ½ width piece of duct tape, firmly tape it again.

To make the hilt:

Cut a piece of pipe insulation about 6 inches long. Cut it lengthwise along the slit. Cut it in half by cutting the other side. Take one piece and cut it in half again lengthwise. (This makes a quarter of the pipe insulation piece for the hilt.)

Cover this hilt piece with a piece of duct tape that is longer by at least 2 inches. Put the rounded side down toward the sticky part of the duct tape.

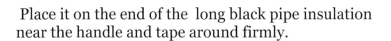

Place it on the end of the long black pipe insulation near the handle and tape around firmly.

Press down on both edges of the duct tape. Using a ½ width piece of duct tape, wrap the shaft just above the hilt piece.

Cap the end of the war hammer by taping over the end. Press down the edges of the duct tape. Turn the war hammer and tape again. Press down the edges to give a finished look.

Cover the shaft with duct tape. It looks good to wrap on the diagonal.

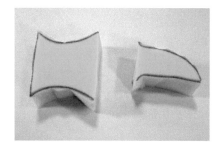

Print and cut out War Hammer Blade and War Hammer Spike patterns. Trace the patterns onto the foam and cut them out.

Place the foam blade piece 3 ½ inches down from the tip of the war hammer.

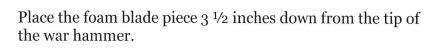

Tape it around the shaft with a long piece of duct tape.

Using a ½ width piece of duct tape, tape diagonally around the edges of the blade on the top and bottom.

Tape around the shaft with a ½ width piece of duct tape on the top and bottom of the blade for strength.

Tape around the base of the blade.

Cover the edges of the blade, carefully shaping as you go. Cover any spots where the foam shows through.

Now for the spike:

Position the spike directly behind the blade on the other side of the shaft. Tape it to the shaft on each side.

Tape the edge of the spike.

Using a ½ width piece of duct tape, tape diagonally on the top and bottom edge of the spike.

Tape the sides of the spike, carefully shaping the edge as you go.

If necessary, take thin strips of duct tape and cover any wrinkles on the edge of the spike.

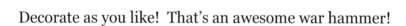

Add tape as needed to make it look good.

Decorate as you like! That's an awesome war hammer!

Mace~

Materials:

2 foot piece of ¾ inch PVC pipe

7 inch piece of PVC pipe insulation

(We use 3/8" thick polyethylene foam, fits ¾" pipe)

1 piece 8 1/2" x 5" x 2" thick foam
(or you can use 1" thick foam 12" x 5")

Duct tape

Scissors/ Marker/ Ruler

Saw (You may need a saw to cut the PVC pipe to size)

   Please Note: This project may require adult help to use the sharp tools.

Directions:

Print and cut out the pattern Mace Spike Ring. Lay the pattern on the foam, trace the spike rings on the foam using a permanent marker and then cut it out.

 You will need 3 spike rings.

 If you are using 2" foam, trace and cut out 2 spike rings. (We'll show you how to get 3 from the two pieces.)

 If you are using 1" foam, trace and cut out 3 spike rings.

Cut out the spike rings.

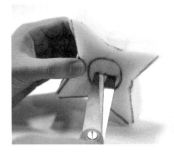

Cut out the inner circle. Poke the scissors in the middle and make small slits. It helps to cut the slits in the shape of an X. Then carefully trim out the rest of the circle.

If you used the 2" thick foam, cut the spike ring in half so it is now 1" thick, see picture.

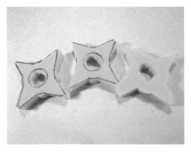

Don't worry if the foam looks a little choppy, the duct tape will cover it up.

Slide the 7 inch piece of pipe insulation onto the PVC pipe, leaving an inch of foam past the end of the PVC pipe.

Tape the pipe insulation to the PVC pipe. Using a ½ width piece of duct tape, firmly tape it again.

Cap the end of the mace by taping over the end. Press down the edges of the duct tape. Turn the mace and tape again. Press down the edges to give a finished look.

Cover the end of the mace with duct tape. Wrap in a spiral direction.

Now to add the spike rings.

Take a piece of duct tape about 4 ½ inches long. Start the tape just below the base of the spike, near the circle. Tape up and over the spike, being careful not to squish the tip. Come down the other side.

Keep in mind as you are taping, to leave a little foam showing near the center circle, so it can stretch as you slide it on.

Press down the tape on the side of the spike, making a neat point.

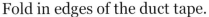

Fold in edges of the duct tape.

Using a ½ width piece of duct tape, wrap around the spike to secure it.

Take a ½ width piece of duct tape and tape from the center of the spike ring up and over the gap between the spikes.

Again, keep in mind as you are taping to leave a little foam showing so it can stretch as you slide it on.

Do this for all four (4) spikes on each of the three spike rings.

Slide the spike ring down onto the silver end of the mace, about an inch from the PVC pipe (or wherever you like it).

Evenly space the other two spike rings onto the mace.

To secure the spike rings, take a ½ width piece of duct tape about 3 inches long and tape from the bottom of the spike ring up and over the gap and on the other side of the spike ring.

Do this to all gaps.

Then take a ½ width piece of duct tape about 6 inches long and tape around the mace *below* the spike ring. Do it again around the mace *above* the spike ring. Do this for all 3 spike rings.

Cap the end of the mace. Place a piece of duct tape over the end. Press the edges down around the PVC pipe.
Wrap another piece of tape around the end to give a smooth finish.

Cover the handle with the color of your choice and decorate to your liking!

Flail~

Materials:

19 inch piece of ¾ inch PVC pipe

Two (2) 1 ½ inch pieces of PVC pipe insulation

(We use 3/8" thick polyethylene foam, fits ¾" pipe)

12" x 10" x 2" foam or scraps

Duct tape

Ruler

Cardboard (at least 10" x 10")

Scissors

Saw (You may need a saw to cut the PVC to size)

Please Note: This project may require adult help to use the sharp tools.

Directions:

Put the pipe insulation pieces onto the PVC pipe.   Put one piece about 6" to 7" from one end and one piece on the end of the PVC pipe.

The pieces should be spaced apart the size of your hand when holding the flail. Fit them where you feel comfortable. See picture.

Wrap a piece of duct tape tightly around the base of the handle half way over the black pipe insulation.

Pinch the duct tape down onto the PVC pipe. Using a ½ width piece of duct tape, wrap around the pinched part.

Repeat this step on both sides of the upper black pipe insulation piece.

Cap the end of the flail handle. Place a piece of duct tape over the end, press in the corners and sides. Turn and do it again with another piece of duct tape. Wrap a ½ width piece of duct tape around the end.

Cap the tip of the flail handle. Take one piece of duct tape, place over the end of the PVC pipe and pinch down the edges. Using a ½ width piece of duct tape, wrap around the end.

For the chain links, cut out eight (8) pieces of 8" x 1" cardboard. Be sure to cut the strips so that the long sections of corrugated inner parts are ***across the 1 inch width of the strip***. This makes the strip stronger and more able to bend in a curve without squishing flat.

Set the cardboard strips aside for now.

Cut one piece of cardboard 7" x 1" for the connector end ring. Cover the cardboard strip completely in duct tape. We suggest wrapping the duct tape around the width several times for strength. It is important that this connector end ring is really strong.

Shape the piece into a curve.

Using a ½ width piece of duct tape, firmly wrap one end of the connector ring to the tip of the flail handle. Wrap around several times, covering the PVC pipe. For extra strength, tape diagonally where the ring meets the tip of the flail handle. (We did it twice.)

Tape down the other end to form the ring, going around the pipe several times with the duct tape.

Tape on the diagonal where the ring meets the flail handle (twice).

Now for the chain links:

Cover the cardboard piece with duct tape. For a smooth finish, use about a 9 inch piece of duct tape. Lay the cardboard onto the tape and fold in the ends and edges. Do it again on the other side of the piece. Now, tape over the ends to finish it off. Crease the piece to form a curve.

Do this to cover all 8 chain link pieces.

To make a closed chain link piece, overlap the ends 1 inch. Use a ½ width piece of duct tape to tape the ends firmly together. It is best to go around several times. Make sure they are well taped to be strong.

Close 3 links.

To form the chain:

Put an open piece of
chain link in the
connector end ring,
overlap and tape
closed.

Put an open piece of chain link
through the closed chain link and
add another closed (finished)
chain link. Tape the chain link
closed.

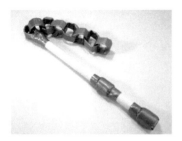

Do this for the rest of the chain but save out one (1) open chain
link piece (to attach to the ball at the end).

Cut the last piece of cardboard 10" x 1". (Again, be sure to
cut the strips so that the long sections of corrugated inner
parts are **across the 1 inch width of the strip**.) Cover
completely in duct tape.

Take a scrap of foam about 5" x 5".
Squish the foam in your hand.
Wrap a ½ width piece of duct tape
around it to make a circle.

Tape it again around the other way to form a "ball". Keep taping around to make a
relatively, round ball. It doesn't have to be perfect; this is duct tape, after all!

Place the end of the 10" strip of covered cardboard on the side of the foam "ball". Firmly tape it on, wrapping around the ball several times. Tape diagonally on the inside where the ball meets the strip.

Repeat with the other side of the strip. This will make the ring to attach the ball to the chain.

Tape another scrap of foam about 4" x 4" lightly onto the little ball (don't squish the foam too much).

Round down the top edges of the foam with tape.

Do again on the other side.

Tape bottom edges to make it more round. Take about a 2/3 width piece of tape and tape across the top of the ball between the ring.

Cover the bottom edges with duct tape.

Cut a piece of foam about 12" x 1 ½" and wrap this foam around the bottom and up the sides of the ball (where the other pieces meet). Take a long piece of duct tape and wrap it around the foam.

Gently, cover the whole ball with duct tape, trying to not squish the foam too much or the ball will be too hard.

Attach the ball to the chain. Slide the open chain link through the ring of the ball and the last chain link. Overlap the link 1" and tape firmly closed.

Decorate the handle as you like. You are done!!

See our Armored Glove Book to make this glove.

44

Shield~

Materials:

Plywood, size and shape of your choice

Four (4) small blocks of wood 3 ½" x 1 ½" x ½"

Cardboard~about 18" x 6"

Duct Tape

Four (4) Screws 1 ½" long (or long enough to go through the blocks of wood, cardboard and plywood)

Saw (to cut plywood if needed)

Screwdriver/ Sandpaper

Scissors/ Ruler   Please Note: This project may require adult help to use the sharp tools.

Directions:

Before you begin cutting the wood, plan the size you want your shield to be. We recommend you measure your arm from the elbow to the knuckles on your hand when you make a fist. The shield should be at least this wide.

Take a piece of plywood and cut to the shape (square, circle, oval, or rectangle) you want for the shield. Either sand the wood or cover the front with duct tape. You may want to add details with duct tape. Usually, we cover the front of the shield with duct tape and sand the back well so that we don't get splinters.

Cut a strip of cardboard 18" long by 4" wide. **: For all cardboard pieces, be sure** to cut the cardboard so the "ridges" (inner corrugated sections) **run across** the narrow width of the piece. This way the piece can bend properly. Cover with duct tape so as to strengthen it. Cut another strip of cardboard 12" long by 2" wide. Also cover with duct tape. Bend up 1 inch on the ends and curve the rest of the piece of cardboard. Do this to both pieces.

The larger piece with go over the forearm. Using your arm, measure where the large piece of cardboard should go on the back of the shield. (You may need a friend to help you with this.)

Tape down the ends of the cardboard piece.

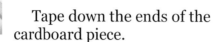

Place a block of wood on the end of that piece and screw down on each end of the block. Do this on both ends of the piece.

If you have a power screw driver, you may want to pre-drill the holes. You can use a regular screwdriver also.

Measure where the smaller piece should go by placing your arm in the large piece. You will grip the smaller piece so place accordingly.

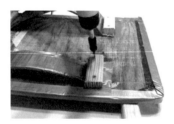

Tape the ends of the cardboard piece to hold it in place. Place a block of wood on the end and screw down on each end of the block. Do this on both ends of the duct tape covered piece.

It should look something like this when it is finished.

The shield is done. Good job!! Decorate as you desire.

Cardboard Shield~

Materials:

Cardboard~whatever size you desire, we used 2 pieces of 24" x 14", plus 13" x 5"

Duct Tape

Scissors

Ruler

Stapler/Staples

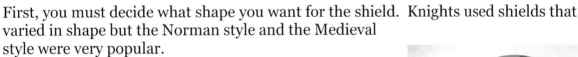

Directions:

First, you must decide what shape you want for the shield. Knights used shields that varied in shape but the Norman style and the Medieval style were very popular.

Cut the cardboard to the shape that you choose. This Norman/Kite based style that we chose is about 24 inches long by about 14 inches wide. You need two (2) of them.

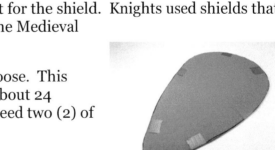

Tape the 2 pieces together spacing the duct tape around the edge of the shield. This is for strength.

Completely cover the edge, taping from the front to the back, all the way around of the shield.

Cover the back of the shield with duct tape.

Decorate the front as desired.

To decorate the shield as shown, tape around the front edge with white, just in from the edge, using small pieces at the curves. Fill in the rest of the area with white duct tape.

To make the cross:

Using a ½ width piece of red duct tape, place a line about 9 inches long in the center of the shield. Use another line 4 inches long for the cross piece.

Use small ½ width pieces of duct tape to cap the ends of the cross for a crusader effect.

To make the straps:

(You may need to modify this to fit the style of shield that you have chosen.)

Please note: For all cardboard pieces, be sure to cut the cardboard so the "ridges" (inner corrugated sections) **run across** the narrow width of the piece. This way the piece can bend properly.

Cut a piece of cardboard 13 inches long by 2 inches wide. Cut another piece of cardboard 13 inches long by 3 inches wide. Leave one inch flat on each end and then crease the pieces so they have a nice curve.

Cover the cardboard strips with duct tape.

Place the strips on the back of the shield where you want them. The wider 3 inch strip should go near the forearm. The narrow strip is for the hand grip. Use a small piece of tape to hold the strips in place while you try it out. Be sure to give your arm plenty of room. Adjust the strips if needed.

Staple the top ends of the strips to the shield many times.   Tape over the top ends. Staple the lower ends of the strips and tape over the ends to cover the staples and reinforce the strips.

Cover any staples that show through the front as needed.

Reinforce the ends by cross taping the duct tape again.

You're done!

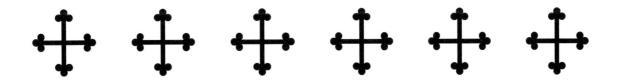

Greathelm~
(Bucket Helmet)

This is an advanced project, not for beginners.

Materials:

Patterns

Cardstock

Cardboard~at least 13" x 9" and 17" x 11"

Duct Tape

Scissors

Clear "scotch" tape

Elastic~about ¾" wide by about 8 or 9 inches long

Stapler/Staples

Please Note: This project may require adult help to use the sharp tools. You may need a helper for some of the steps.

Directions:

Please note: For all cardboard pieces, be sure to cut the cardboard so the "ridges" (inner corrugated sections) **run across** the narrow width of the piece. This way the piece can bend properly.

Print the helmet pieces on cardstock and cut them out.

You will need the Upper Helmet, Back of Helmet, Greathelm Template (optional, see instructions) and Top of Greathelm. . (If you want the helmet in a smaller size, try minimizing the patterns on a copy machine.)

Please note: You will need to print the Greathelm template and cut it out. Then attach the side pieces to the main section as shown in the picture.

Tape together the upper helmet pieces at the center front with the "scotch" tape.

Tape together the side edges at the top of the helmet pieces.

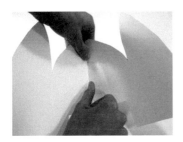  

Put a piece of duct tape at the lower side of the helmet, next to the eyehole.

Fold the duct tape under on the straight edge but trim the curved edge with a scissors.

Cover the helmet neatly with duct tape, moving up the helmet as you work.

Crease the duct tape at the ridge on the side of the helmet and trim with a scissors.

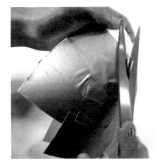  

Cover the other side of the helmet as well.

Cover the inside of the helmet with duct tape.

Trace the back of the helmet piece onto cardboard and cut out.

Be sure to cut the cardboard so the "ridges" (inner corrugated sections) **run across** the helmet piece. This way the piece can bend properly.

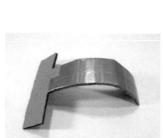

Bend the long upper section of the back helmet piece into a curve to form around the head.

Cover upper section with duct tape inside and out.

Also bend the lower side sections into a curve and cover with duct tape inside and out.

Attach the back helmet piece to the top (crown) of the helmet with duct tape. Secure with 2 staples and then cover them with duct tape.

Cut elastic into two (2) 4 ½ inch pieces. Attach elastic to upper helmet by stapling and then covering with duct tape. **Please note:** Staple away from the inside so the point of the staples are not near the skin.

Tape the other loose end of elastic to the back of the helmet piece.

Try on the helmet and adjust fit if necessary.

Staple elastic to back of helmet and cover staples with duct tape on both sides.

Greathelm Crown (Top)

Trace and cut the Greathelm Crown (top) out of cardboard.

Staple the Greathelm Crown piece to top of helmet at the back helmet piece and in the center of the circle.

To add extensions on the lower sides of the main helmet, cut two (2) 3" wide x 4" pieces of cardboard. Staple an extension to each side of the main helmet and cover with duct tape. (The 4" goes the longway.)

Cut a 12" x 1" piece of cardboard for a chin guard. Bend into a curve.

Try on helmet. Place ends of the chin guard on the bottom edges of the helmet. Adjust fit. The guard should go over your chin with plenty of space so it doesn't touch the face. Then tape firmly in place on the sides, inside and outside.

Now we will use a series of strips to make the "bucket" part.

Cut a piece of cardboard 12" x 2". Bend into a curve. Place on the center front. Tape the strip to the circle at the crown and to the chin guard.

Cut two (2) pieces of cardboard 11 ½" x 2". Bend them into a curve. These pieces go on either side of the center piece. Tape one end to the chin guard close to the center piece. Hold the strip up to the crown and trim the end so it has a slight angle to match the edge of the crown. Then tape the strip to the crown. (Do again on the other side of center)

Cut two (2) pieces of cardboard 10" x 1 ¾". Bend them into a curve. Moving farther to the sides, tape one end to the chin guard. Hold the piece up to the crown and trim the end so it has a slight angle. Then tape it to the crown. (Do again on the other side.)

You should have 5 strips of cardboard making a bucket shape over the face of the helmet.

Cut slivers of cardboard and tape them between the long strips. Tape on the inside and the outside. Cover the main strips of cardboard with duct tape as you go.

Cover the outside completely in duct tape, including the circle on top (the crown).

Using a pencil, poke through the helmet from the back where the eyehole should be.

You can design your own eyehole decoration or you may use the Greathelm template.

Print the Greathelm template. Cut out the template and the 2 side pieces. Tape the side pieces to the main template as shown in the photo with "scotch" tape. Place the template over the front of the helmet. Make sure the eyehole lines up with the hole you poked with the pencil.

Trace the eyehole onto the helmet and cut out the eyehole. This may be difficult so get some help if you need it.

Trace the template onto cardboard and cut it out around the outside and also cut out the eyehole. Place this on the front of the helmet. Line up the eyehole. Tape it in place with duct tape. Make sure to press around the cardboard to define the edges. Tape around the eyehole for a finished look. You can duct tape the inside of the "bucket" as you desire.

Decorate as desired. You can add some black squares of duct tape for "air holes", if you like!

Optional: Add a cardboard plume to the top.

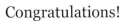

Congratulations!

You are now a master armorer!!

Visored Helmet~

Materials:

Patterns

Cardstock

Cardboard~at least 13" x 9"

Duct Tape

Scissors

Clear "scotch" tape

Elastic~about ¾" wide by about 8 or 9 inches long

Stapler/Staples

Ruler

    Please Note: This project may require adult help to use the sharp tools.

Directions:

Print the helmet pieces on **cardstock** and cut them out.

You will need the helmet pieces: Upper helmet piece, Lower Visor, Forehead Visor, and Back of Helmet. (If you want the helmet in a smaller size, try minimizing the patterns on a copy machine.)

Please note: For all cardboard pieces, be sure to cut the cardboard so the "ridges" (inner corrugated sections) **run across** the narrow width of the piece. This way the piece can bend properly.

Please note: You will need to print two (2) of each of the visor pieces and put them together to make the visor piece. The visors are 13 inches long and wouldn't fit onto a regular piece of paper. ☺

Tape together the upper helmet pieces at the center front with the "scotch" tape.

Tape together the side edges at the top of the helmet pieces.

Put a piece of duct tape at the lower side of the helmet.

Fold the duct tape under on the straight edge but trim the curved edge with a scissors.

Cover the helmet neatly with duct tape, moving up the helmet as you work.

Crease the duct tape at the ridge on the side of the helmet and trim with a scissors.

Cover the other side of the helmet as well. Cover the inside of the helmet with duct tape.

Trace the back of the helmet piece onto cardboard and cut out.

Be sure to cut the cardboard so the "ridges" (inner corrugated sections) **run across** the helmet piece. This way the piece can bend properly.

Bend the long upper section of the back helmet piece into a curve to form around the head.

Cover upper section with duct tape inside and out.

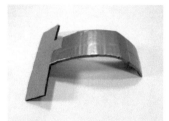 

Also bend the lower side sections into a curve and cover with duct tape inside and out.

Attach the back helmet piece to the top (crown) of the helmet with duct tape inside and outside. Secure with 2 staples and then cover them with duct tape.

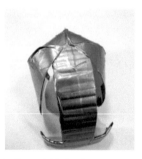

Cut elastic into two (2) 4 ½ inch pieces. Attach elastic to upper helmet by stapling and then covering with duct tape. **Please note:** Staple away from the inside so the point of the staples are not near the skin.

 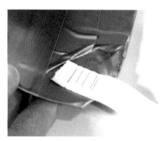

Tape the other loose end of elastic to the back of the helmet piece. Try on the helmet and adjust fit if necessary.

Staple elastic to back of helmet and cover staples with duct tape.

Trace the visor patterns onto cardboard and cut out. Again, cut the cardboard so the "ridges" (inner corrugated sections) **run across** the visor piece. This way the piece can bend properly.

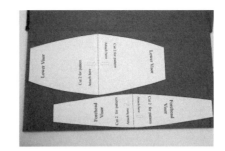

Bend the visor pieces in half. Cover the visor pieces with duct tape inside and out.

Put on the helmet and place the forehead visor, the narrow one, over the forehead above the eyes, just so you can see out. Tape at the sides.

Put on the helmet and place the lower visor over the lower part of the face and helmet edges. Adjust so there is a small slit to see through. This will vary from person to person so you will have to find out what works best for you.

Our slit was about ¾ of an inch. Tape sides firmly inside and out.

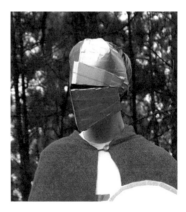

Cover any spots with duct tape as needed.

We do recommend that you cover the visor pieces before you attach them to the helmet. It is just easier that way. Our pictures show a different order because we were creating the helmet as we went and so learned a few tricks along the way! ☺

Leg Armor~

Materials:

Cardboard (see instructions)

Elastic, ¾ inch wide (see instructions) (We used black elastic)

Duct Tape

Velcro 2" wide by about 9 inches long

Stapler/ Staples

Scissors

Ruler

Marker

Please Note: This project may require adult help to use the sharp tools.

Directions:

To find how much cardboard you need, measure from the top of the knee cap to the ankle. This is the **length** of the leg armor.

Measure around the calf of the leg at the widest part. (Save this number for later) Divide this number in half. This is the **width** of the leg armor. (Basically, the front of the leg.) You will need two (2) pieces of cardboard this length and width for the leg armor. You can make them any size you wish, these are just our recommendations.

Note about the cardboard: Be sure the "grains" (inner corrugated parts of the cardboard) run lengthwise on the leg armor. Otherwise, you will have trouble bending and shaping them to the leg.

Elastic: Measure around the calf and the ankle. Add these numbers. Multiply by 2. This is the length of the elastic that you will need for the leg armor. Keep these numbers; you will need them again later.

Hold the piece of cardboard up to your leg. Draw a line across the cardboard near the widest part of your calf.

You want to make it thinner at the bottom, near the ankle so it looks authentic. Make some lines to show where you will cut it thinner. Just eye-ball it.

Then give it a bit of an artistic curl near the edges on the top half. Round the top edges, too.

Cut out on the lines.

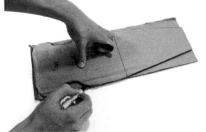

The second piece is easy. Just trace the lines from the first one and cut out.

Bend the cardboard by forming it over your leg and keep creasing it so it stays in the curved shape.

Put one strip of duct tape across on the outside at the widest part (where you drew the line across).

Then tape inside, across the width of the cardboard, a couple strips of duct tape to keep the curve.

Continue taping the inside until it is covered.

Tape horizontally across the entire outside of the leg armor piece.

Cut a piece of velcro 2 ½ inches long.

Place the soft side of the velcro piece on the inside edge of the leg armor at the widest point.

Tape down the inside edge of velcro with a full piece of duct tape, covering about a ½ inch of the velcro.

Tape again, using a ½ width piece of duct tape.

Using a ¼ width piece of duct tape, firmly tape the velcro on the edge near the outside of the leg armor. Tape again a couple more times, pressing over the edge.

Staple firmly on the edges through the duct tape and again in the middle of the velcro piece. Cover the staples with duct tape.

On the front of the leg armor, cover with duct tape any staples that may have poked through.

Cut a length of elastic the width of your calf. (Remember the calf measurement number you saved?)

Take the "pokey" piece of velcro that you have left, place it "pokey" part facing out and staple it to the end of the elastic piece. Be sure to staple with the elastic piece on top so the points of the staple are facing the leg armor when it is fastened!

Cover the elastic and velcro end with a piece of duct tape on the elastic side. See picture. This side touches the leg.

Tape down the loose end of elastic on the other side of the leg armor. Try on the leg armor, wrapping the elastic around the back of the leg and attaching the velcro together. Adjust the fit, tighten or loosen the elastic as needed.

When it fits well, staple through the elastic and tape several times. Cover the staples on the front of the leg armor with duct tape.

Repeat for the ankle strap. You can cut the velcro a little smaller for the ankle strap. We used about 1 ½ inches long for the velcro at the ankle. And, cut the elastic the size of the ankle.

Repeat all directions for the second leg armor piece. **Note: When making the second leg armor piece put the velcro and elastic pieces on the opposite side so that you have a matched pair! ☺**

Decorate as you desire.

The leg armor is finished! Now you are ready for battle!

Costumes

Tunic~

Materials:

Some sort of fabric-knit, sheets, cotton, or whatever you have
Belt or material for a sash
Scissors
Sewing machine or needle and thread
Measuring tape or ruler

Directions:

First determine the size you will need. Most knights' tunics went down to the knees and had sleeves, often long sleeves.
Width of fabric: The size of your fabric may determine the width. For long sleeves, spread the arms out and measure wrist to wrist. Make it wide enough in the main body so that you can slip it over your head and shoulders, get the arms out of the armholes and freely walk.

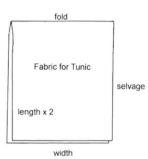

Length of fabric: Measure from the shoulder to the knees for the length. You will need twice the length to make the tunic. If you have enough fabric, double over the fabric so you won't need to sew a seam across the shoulders.

Double over the fabric as shown in the picture, putting the **right sides together**. Cut a hole for the head to go through on the fold in the center. If the fabric is not long enough to double, lay the two pieces right side together, cut out and sew a seam across the top edge.

To make sleeves in your tunic, make a "T" shape of fabric. Give plenty of room in the arms so they can move freely. Be sure the main body of the tunic is wide enough so that you can get it on and get the arms through the sleeves. (You could measure around the person with their arms at their sides and add a little more.)

The No-Sew Option is to just pull the tunic over the head (right side out) and use a belt to keep it around the waist.

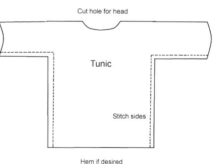

The Sewing Option is to sew up the sides and down the sleeves. Hem the bottom of the tunic and the ends of the sleeves if desired. When finished sewing, turn the tunic **right side out.**

Some children are small and the hole in the neck will gap too much. Just add a button and loop at the back of the neck to close it a little. See Cloak instructions.

Use a belt or cut a strip of fabric to wrap around the waist. An oversize t-shirt would also work for smaller knights. And, yes, the red cross on our tunic is red duct tape!!

Cloak~

Materials:
Some sort of fabric-knit, sheets, curtains, cotton, or whatever you have
Button
Thin piece of elastic, ribbon, or string
Couple of pins
Scissors
Needle and thread
Scissors

Directions:
Determine the size of cape that you need. Do you want a cloak that goes down to the knees or almost to the floor? Knights' cloaks usually went down to the ankles. That is your length measurement plus an inch to turn over at the neck. The width of your fabric may determine your width of the cloak; otherwise decide how wide you want it. The knight's cloak was usually wide enough to wrap around himself like a blanket, if needed.

Cut your fabric to size. If you are using a fabric that will fray, you may want to hem the sides first.

Fold over an inch the top edge which will go by the neck. Try it on. Clasp the cape closed a few inches down from the front of the neck; this where you will attach the button and elastic (ribbon). Mark it on both sides with a pin. Sew on the button on one side. Measure a small piece of elastic (ribbon) around the button so you can still get it on and off. Stitch elastic (ribbon) on both ends to the cape at the mark.

Throw over the shoulders and button at the neck.

Money Pouch~

Materials:
Fabric: see Directions
String, rope, ribbon, shoe lace or whatever you have.
Safety pin
Scissors
Sewing machine or needle and thread
Option: Leg from a pair of cut off pants

Directions:

You can make a money pouch out of almost anything. If you want a money pouch that is a bit fancier, you can use fabric. We just happened to have a scrap of velour that we used for a pouch. Knit fabric won't fray and is easier but any durable fabric will work.

Determine the size of pouch that you want. For example, if you want a pouch that is 5" x 7", allowing for seam allowances and the casing for the drawstring, cut two (2) squares of 6" x 8 ½". You can also cut a long rectangle and just fold over so that you eliminate one seam. The rectangle would be 6" x 16".

Put the right sides together and sew up the seams leaving one 6" side open (use ½" seam). Turn over 1" at the opening. Stitch around using a small seam of about ¼". On the side or center front, make a small cut in the casing only on the front piece big enough for the drawstring to go through.

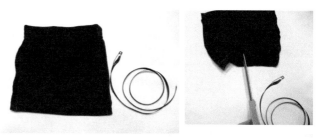

Cut your drawstring to at least twice the length of your opening or top of the pouch. In this example, the opening is 10" after sewing, so the drawstring should be 20" long. Put the safety pin in the end of the drawstring and push it through the casing.

A leg from a pair of pants that was cut off into shorts can be made into a pouch. Cut to the size you want. Sew one end. Cut small slits about an inch apart and weave your drawstring in and out through the slits. If you don't have any, thrift stores and yard sales often have pants for cheap.

Coin Money for Ransom~

Materials:
Aluminum foil
Something heavy like a hammer or shoe

Directions:

Take a small piece of aluminum foil about twice the size you want the coin to be and fold in the edges to make a circle. It's all right if it is not perfectly round, ancient money wasn't perfect either. Press down firmly against a hard surface and then hammer flat with the heel of a shoe or a hammer.

Mark the coins with designs or figures so you know which coins belong to you. You can also make a money pouch to keep your money in while you are battling. See instructions for money pouch.

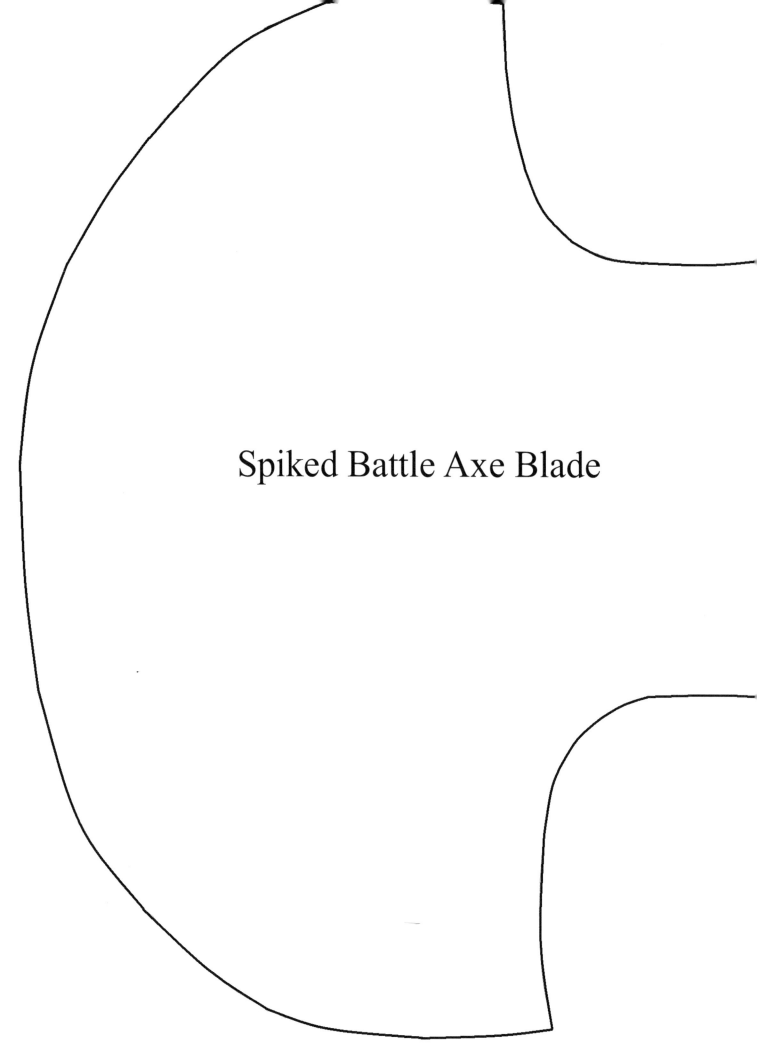

Spiked Battle Axe Blade

Spiked Battle Axe Spike

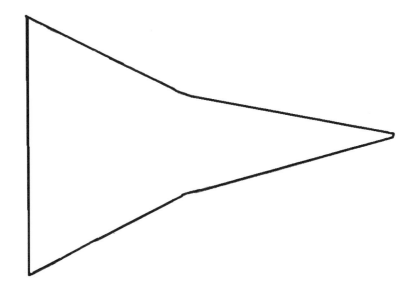

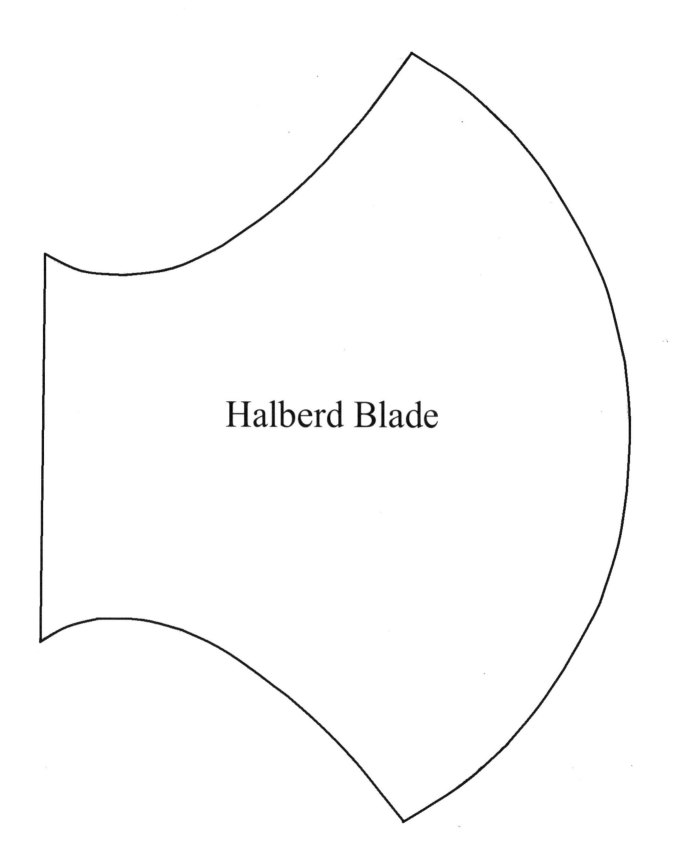

Halberd Blade

Halberd Spike

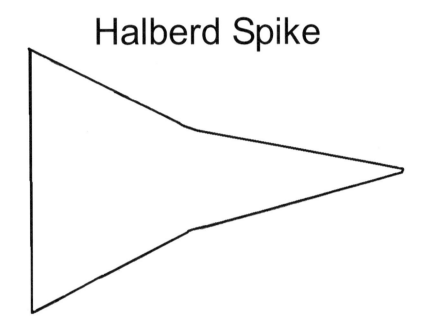

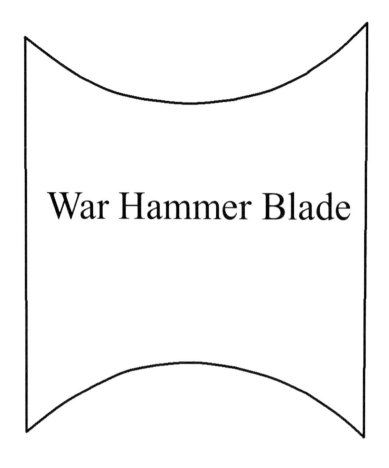

War Hammer Blade

War Hammer Spike

Mace Spike Ring

Cut 3
of foam

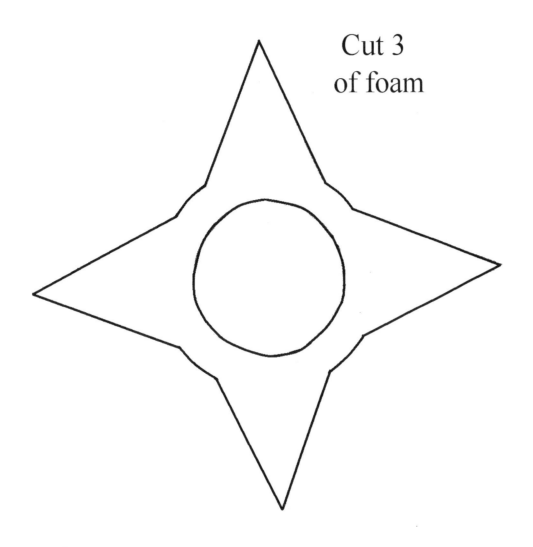

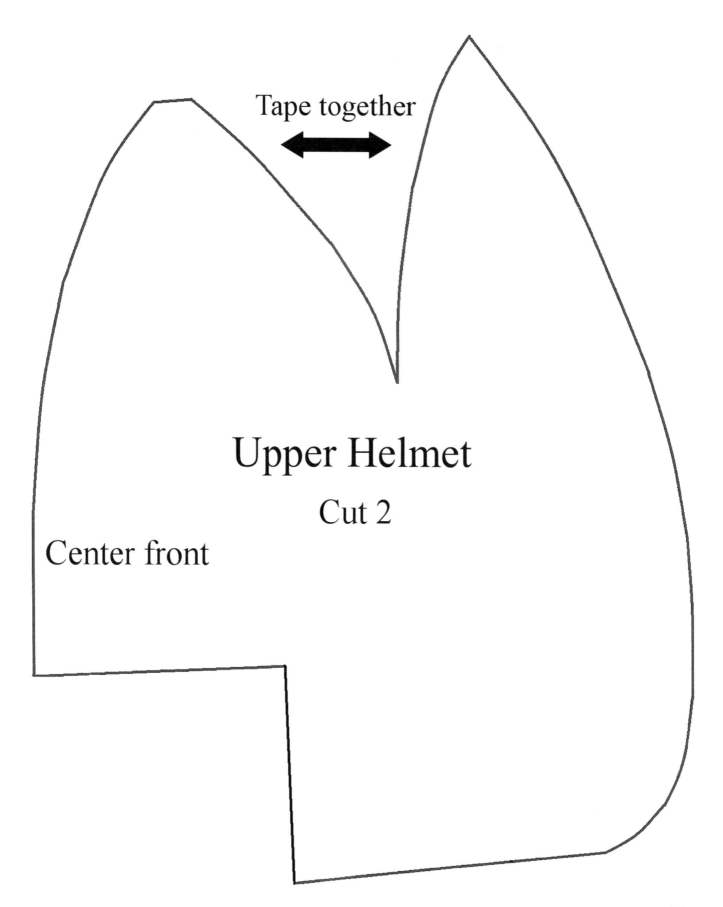

Tape together

Upper Helmet

Cut 2

Center front

Cut 1
of
cardboard

Back of Helmet

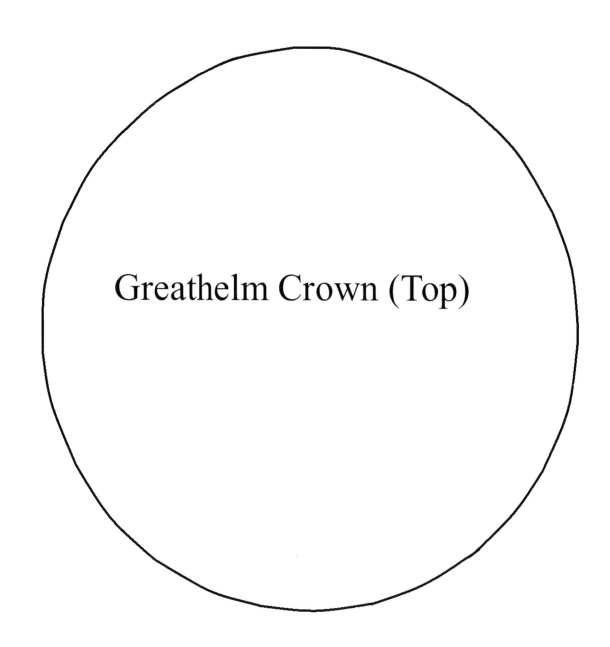

Greathelm Crown (Top)

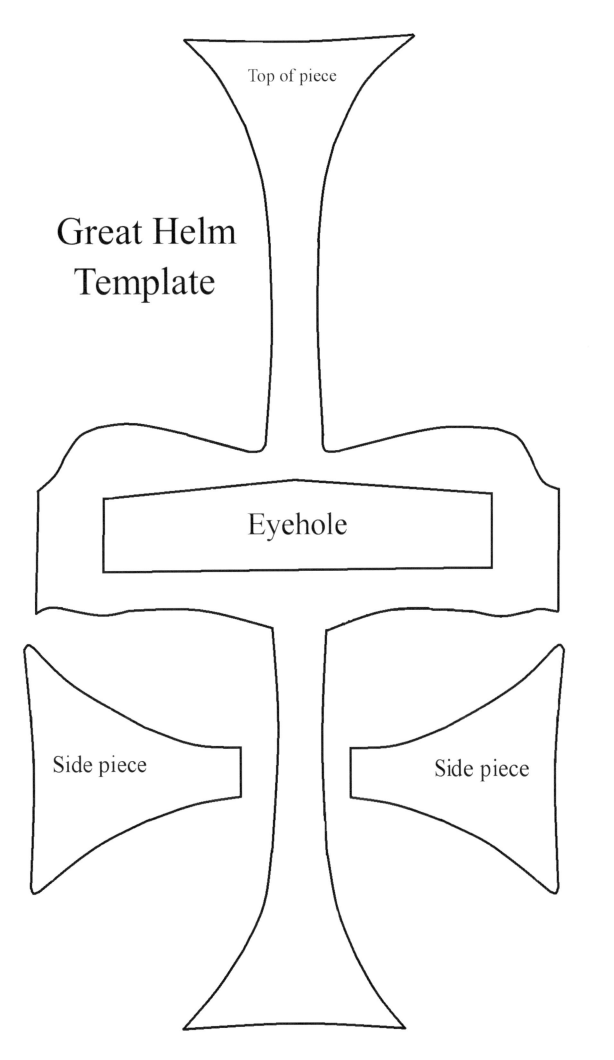

Top of piece

Great Helm
Template

Eyehole

Side piece

Side piece

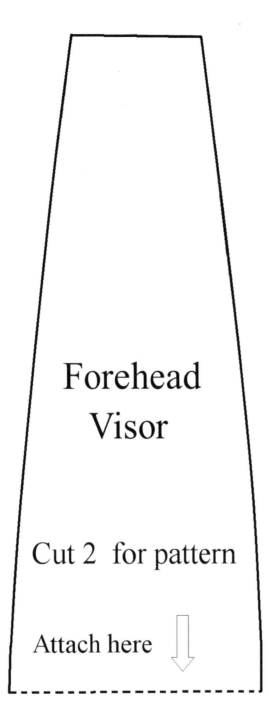

Forehead
Visor

Cut 2 for pattern

Attach here

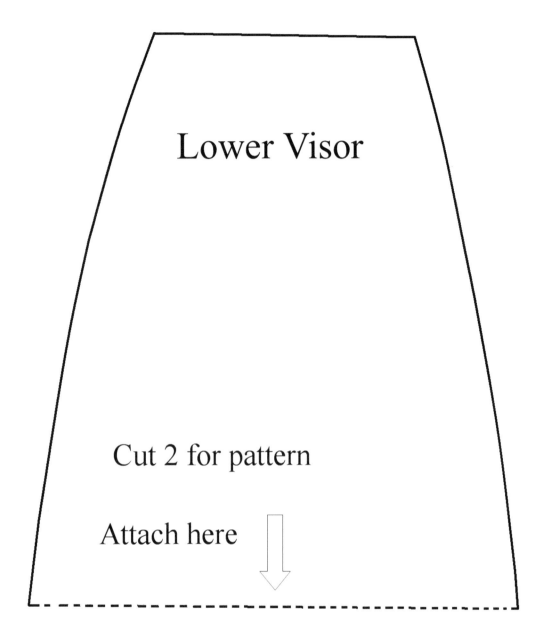

Lower Visor

Cut 2 for pattern

Attach here

Visit our website
www.warfarebyducttape.com for more information.

Also available from Warfare by Duct Tape:

Made in United States
Troutdale, OR
01/01/2025